Jim Thornber gave me a gift; he allowe[...]
the grieving moments following the d[...]
I admire Jim for writing about his ex[...]
cess. Very few people have the energy a[...] [...] emotional well-being
to gather their thoughts and feelings as quickly as Jim. Excellently
written, this book will assist many people facing significant loss in
their lives. Pastors will want this book as a tool to assist those grieving in their communities. I am grateful to Jim for sharing his life
with us as we all search for understanding in the sad moments of
our lives.

DR. LOU SHIREY
Director of Thriving in Ministry Program
International Pentecostal Holiness Church

Pastor Jim's personal story of the sudden loss of his beloved wife
Barbara is both timely and moving. As a seasoned writer, he leads
the reader through a narrative that is at times both heart-wrenching
and celebratory. His story is a poignant reflection of the pain of this
temporal world and the hope we have in the Eternal. For those who
feel hopeless and overwhelmed in their grief, Jim's story offers hope,
concrete examples of helpful actions, and the assurance of God's
sustaining love and comfort.

DR. MELODY D. PALM
Licensed Clinical Psychologist, Professor of Counseling Evangel University

Jim Thornber's book about his experiences during the first forty days
after the loss of Barbara, his wife and best friend, is a gift to all who
are grieving the loss of a loved one. It is a deeply personal, emotional, and hope-giving book. I found it helpful in many places and at
many levels, and I particularly appreciated Jim's sharing of his inner

dialogue when well-meaning friends would offer attempts to provide comfort.

GARY W. MOON, M.DIV., PH.D.
Founding Executive Director, Martin Institute
and Dallas Willard Center, Westmont College
Author of *Apprenticeship with Jesus, Becoming Dallas Willard*

WOW! That's my response after reading the manuscript for my dear friend and fellow minister of the Gospel, Jim Thornber. *Better with Every Breath* is Jim's mantra after the death of his WOW (you will understand after you read the book), but these four words should be a mantra for each of us throughout our lives. Through my tears and smiles while reading, I pondered my own marriage, life, and witness, as you will do. Thank you, Jim, for sharing your intimate, innermost feelings and observations following Barb's passing.

BISHOP RANDELL O. DRAKE
New Horizons Ministries Conference
International Pentecostal Holiness Church

Our world continues traveling through tough times. We wake up to face days of sadness and uncertainty. But with every news report and every statistic, with alarming updates and unanswered questions, with every long wait and honest conversation, there is a story. A real life story of how life can end. A painful story of endurance and questions and uncertainty and—even when it seems impossible—hope.

James Thornber offers us one of those raw stories including hope in the air. I read his story and elected to inhale that hope. I reflected on my own painful stories, and continued breathing that therapeutic air.

His authentic confessions give us glimpses at better days—even during sad seasons of grief. As we travel, the hope James Thornber offers can bring healing and peace even during times like these. I am sad about his grief. But I am thankful for the hope he brings to us through his book.

CHRIS MAXWELL
Pastor, Author, Poet

Telling writing is when we read something we've always known, but can't put into words. In this memoir, Jim Thornber reminds us joy and sorrow are parallel paths in life. Let healing and hope take hold of you.

STEVE GRANT
Anchor Noon & 6pm
KY3, Inc
Springfield, MO 65807
Chapter President, MID-AMERICA EMMY AWARDS St. Louis, MO

Today it gives me great pleasure to endorse Jim's book, *Better with Every Breath*. Pastor Jim has captured on these pages glimpses of the most difficult journey of his life. His ability to express his raw emotions concerning Barbara's passing gives the reader an understanding that will help them through their difficult parts of life's journey. This book helps us know that our journey is not yet complete, but there is hope and strength for us all as we encounter life's challenges. He gives great insight into the necessity to choose to act and react to life in a Christlike manner.

PASTOR KEITH BUTLER
Church on the Hill
Berryville, Arkansas

In *Better with Every Breath*, James Thornber courageously, transparently, and masterfully weaves personal stories with great lessons to help readers who are struggling with the severe pain of loss. This book intersects God's grace, goodness, and love through the journey of grief.

REVEREND EDDIE RENTZ
National Church Spokesperson, Convoy of Hope
Vice President, National Hispanic Christian Leadership Conference

When there are "no words" to adequately express the depth of loss, this powerful book somehow finds them. Written with the honesty only someone who's traveled the path of grief can give, you'll discover the hope your soul longs for as you learn to breathe again. I highly recommend Jim's book!

DONNA JONES
National Speaker and Author of *Seek: A Woman's Guide to Meeting God*

As we read Jim Thornber's book, we realized this was the kind of book we could share with people who need a road map to help with grief when they lose a loved one. The field of psychotherapy, over the past few years, has begun to recognize that gratitude plays a major role in maintaining mental health during a crisis. This was not a new thought to Jim, but a necessary spiritual discipline that is helping him navigate through his journey of grief.

REVEREND STAN MCCABE AND MARIE MCCABE, MA, LMFT, BCN
IPHC Clergy Care Directors, New Horizons Ministry

Far too many people who have experienced loss feel trapped by their grief, enslaved by their loss, and defined by their pain, which is why I can't wait for people to read *Better with Every Breath*. It's replete with interesting yet raw stories of a courageous man (Jim Thornber) walking through the early stages of grief, but it's also incredibly practical and life-giving. You are about to embark on a life-changing journey to discover the depths of God's help, hope, and healing.

CRAIG BUTLER
Executive Small Group and Discipleship Pastor,
Victory Church, Lakeland, FL

Jim Thornber writes from a deep place that few of us dare to explore. Jim takes us on a practical and at times painful journey into the depths of grief. While he writes from a place of grief and pain, there is an overarching commitment to the Sovereignty of God. This book offers a powerful perspective that I desperately need. It also gives me a better understanding of eternity. Exceedingly rich with wisdom, *Better with Every Breath* is for everyone who desires to more significantly practice the power of gratefulness—particularly on the hardest of days. I highly recommend this book for anyone seeking a deeper, fuller, richer understanding of the power of gratefulness in the midst of a broken world.

JIMMY DODD
Founder and President, PastorServe
Author of *Survive or Thrive, Six Relationships Every Pastor Needs, Pastors are People Too* and *What Great Ministry Leaders Get Right*

As a man who loves his wife in the same way Jim loved Barbara, this story travels deep into my psyche and soul. I couldn't help but place myself in Jim's shoes. *Better with Every Breath* is as much therapeutic as it is directional. It's the perfect resource for pastors, counselors, or the caring neighbor who is trying to find the right words for someone facing sudden loss. More than an invitation to peer inside one man's bereavement journey, *Better with Every Breath* is a beautiful story-map toward wholeness.

SCOTT HAGAN, PH.D.
President, North Central University, Minneapolis, MN

BETTER
WITH
EVERY
BREATH

THE JOURNEY FROM LOSS
TO LIVING AGAIN

James Thornber

HIGHERLIFE
PUBLISHING & MARKETING

In Memory of Barbara

Scripture quotations are taken from the *Holy Bible, New Living Translation*,
copyright © 1996, 2004, 2007, 2013 by Tyndale House Foundation. Used by
permission of Tyndale House Publishers, Inc., Carol Stream, Illinois 60188.
All rights reserved.

HigherLife Publishing & Marketing
PO Box 623307
Oviedo, FL 32762
AHigherLife.com

Better with Every Breath/ James Thornber -- 1st ed.
ISBN 978-1-954533-06-6 Paperback
ISBN 978-1-954533-07-3 eBook

Library of Congress Control Number: 2021901361

Cover and interior design by Jonathan Lewis/Jonlin Creative

Cover art: Autumn Leaf, Photo 136894431 © Marijus Auruskevicius
Dreamstime.com

10 9 8 7 6 5 4 3 2 1

Contents

Contents

Foreword

IWAS SHOCKED WHEN I heard the news that Barbara Thornber had died. I knew that she, and her husband Jim, were battling the coronavirus, but was under the impression they both had improved.

Besides the shock at the news of her death, I had two other visceral responses. The first was a mental picture of her: a slender woman with bright eyes and an inviting smile. The second was the emotional response of sorrow for her husband, family, church family, and all of us who knew her.

As a minister, I have read many books about death and dying, including some mentioned by Jim in this book. Many of these books are testimonies of the experience of walking through the valley of the shadow of death. While the psalmist David wrote of that valley in Psalm 23, he told us that through the Lord's shepherding presence, we did not have to fear evil. In Jim's testimony of their life together, and her unexpected passing, we hear a voice of sorrow, but not a voice afraid of evil.

I also found myself thinking about this book's timing as Jim continues to walk through grief. Often those who write about a loved one's passing do so after some time when grief has completed much of its process. Rarely, someone writes so poignantly amid such sorrow. As you read, you will sense the emotional rawness. But you will not be embarrassed or put off by it. The Holy Spirit has enabled this grieving widower to share a story of shock, pain, and sorrow in a way that invites us to appreciate more fully the power of love.

Ecclesiastes 7:1 is a verse I've often pondered: "A good name is better than precious ointment, and the day of death than the day of one's birth" (NKJV). I've often used this verse as a minister speaking at a funeral or memorial service.

Solomon, who composed the beautiful love Song of Solomon, and the discerning view of life from the standpoint of many years in Ecclesiastes, used the same Hebrew word for ointment in three places in those two books.

Besides the citation above, it is also used in Ecclesiastes 10:1, again about death. Like dead flies in the ointment that ruin the carefully prepared aroma, folly can change the atmosphere of "one respected for wisdom and honor." Thankfully, in Jim and Barb's life, we smell the aroma of Christ, as the Apostle Paul phrased it in 2 Corinthians 2:16. Their life together lingers as "the aroma of life leading to life."

But returning to Ecclesiastes 7:1, it is the "good name" of a person that "is better than precious ointment." The second clause explains why that statement is true. The day of death contains the history of the person who has died. They have left memories, love, and a legacy that are memorialized with family and friends. It is on the day of death that we can look back and genuinely say, "She was a good person. She has a good name."

We cannot speak that way on the day of birth. That day is filled with potential. But no one knows what will indeed come of that potential. At the day of birth, we dream, we hope.

But on the day of death, we know. Of course, our knowledge is limited to any person's life. Only God and eternity reveals the full story. But we usually know enough.

Barb and Jim found themselves living in the presence and power of the One whose "name is like ointment poured forth" (Song of Solomon 1:3). The connection of our name, whether good or bad, is ultimately based on our relationship to the One whose name is healing, calming, cleansing ointment. That Name is an ointment that soothes and smooths, an ointment that prepares one for what is coming.

So along with Jim, I invite you to enter into the aroma of this book. It is an aroma that will bring you tears, bring you hope, and bring you joy.

Dr. A.D. Beacham, Jr.
General Superintendent
International Pentecostal Holiness Church
Oklahoma City, Oklahoma USA

"And even in our sleep, pain which cannot forget

falls drop by drop upon the heart

until, in our own despair, against our will,

comes wisdom through the awful grace of God."

AESCHYLUS

Introduction

FORTY DAYS AGO, my wife and my soul mate, my beloved best friend for over twenty-six years, died of complications from COVID-19. Barbara Elizabeth Shelley Thornber—I called her my "B.E.S.T."—was sixty-six years old.

Today is also the first day since her death that I have not shed a tear. Tomorrow may be different. I'll see. (It was.)

These forty days have been filled with times of worshiping on the mountain of God as Moses did *and* with the temptation Jesus faced of turning away from God in the desert. He did not turn away. Neither have I. I've experienced highs and lows, tears and laughter, sleepless nights and the blessed one or two times I woke with my alarm. Although this sounds like a cacophony of feelings and emotions, it's really more like a harmony where body and soul, mind and spirit are all trying to relearn their relationship with one another in a time of joy and sorrow, gratitude and mourning, life and death.

This book is not a journal, but a journey. I'm writing now while the emotions are raw, the lessons are clear, the insights still shine, and the much-needed grace and mercies of God are current, fresh, and sufficient every morning. Now is the time to share how, through a decision to choose gratitude *before* I faced a potentially devastating event, God has comforted me with His magnificent goodness.

I know some may read this within their own first forty days of loss and grief. Others, while not facing the death of a spouse, may find themselves mourning the death of a marriage through divorce or the loss of a child or parent. Still others have faced months or years of indescribable loss and sorrow and wonder if life will ever get better. It will. God specializes in rebuilding lives.

During her surgery but before the doctors told me that Barbara had died, I knew I had to make a decision and a vow. I promised God, through the tears, that I would rejoice in His sovereign goodness come what may. That heart-wrenching conscious decision, that vow to my Sovereign Lord, has never failed to bring me closer, day by day, to a better understanding of His magnificent love.

Now, when people ask me how I'm doing because they don't know what else to say, my usual response is, "Better with every breath." This tells them, and reminds me, that I'm further along in the healing process than I was yesterday, but even today I'm still not where I will one day be. I've often told my congregation, "If you're still breathing, God's not finished with you yet." I am still breathing.

Yesterday, I realized I have sad days and I have better days, and counselors have told me to expect this for eight months to a year. Somehow, I must face and live through the year of "firsts." Our first anniversary alone. The first Christmas without her handing out gifts. The first Father's Day I don't get a card from Barbara. The first time driving to see the family without her in the car.

Breathe, Jim.

Breath by breath turns into day by day. Forty days into the grief process, I know I haven't arrived where God is taking me next. In fact, I don't even know what "arrived" will look like. I'm sure it will be different for all of us. But I know I serve a magnificent and good God who also knows what it means to lose a loved one. He called Him "Son." God understands our emotions, thoughts, unspeakable pain, and questions about tomorrow. King David wrote, "O LORD, you have examined my heart and know everything about me" (Ps. 139:1). That helps when I feel like I know so little about myself and don't even know how to communicate *that* to God. Mercifully, He already knows.

I'm glad the author of Hebrews reminds us that we can rely upon a Savior who loved us to death when he wrote:

> So then, since we have a great High Priest who has entered heaven, Jesus the Son of God, let us hold firmly to what we believe. This High Priest of ours understands our weaknesses, for he faced all of the same testings we do, yet he did not sin. So let us come boldly to the throne of our gracious God. There we will receive his mercy, and we will find grace to help us when we need it most. (Hebrews 4:14-16)

"The discipline of gratitude is the explicit effort

to acknowledge that all I am and have is

given to me as a gift of love, a gift

to be celebrated with joy."

HENRI NOUWEN

Choosing Joy

ON AUGUST 23, 2020, Barbara woke up and told me that she was not feeling well. The coronavirus was and still is a hot topic, and in order to be safe, we both went to the hospital to be tested. Her test came back positive, but I tested negative. Because we only have one bathroom in the house, true isolation wasn't possible for me and, five days later, I tested positive.

For the next few weeks, we did what many couples did in quarantine—we worked around the house, took early morning walks, put together a puzzle, and played lots of Scrabble® (she finally won our last game and was delighted to share that victory with her mom). When the Health Department declared us free to resume our normal activities, I went back to work. Barbara had already retired.

Although we thought we were both over the coronavirus, we didn't know it had settled deep into her lungs. This produced a clot that put her heart in distress. Clots also settled in her right leg, which started to go numb, and that's what sent us to the local emergency room in Independence, Kansas.

Our doctor directed us to St. John's Hospital in Tulsa. While Barbara was transported in an ambulance, I followed in our car. Because they put her in full COVID-19 isolation and the hospital closed the waiting rooms, I spent the next five hours sitting in our Toyota Rav 4 in the parking garage.

A cardiologist and a vascular surgeon consulted to determine if Barbara's heart was strong enough to handle the removal of the clots from her leg. They weren't 100% sure her heart could endure the surgery, but they knew she would lose her foot, if not her leg, if they didn't try. They informed Barb of the diagnosis and the procedure, then called me and told me the situation. I agreed they should try.

A few minutes after I talked to the doctor, Barbara called me from her cell phone. I asked her how she was doing with all this information about the surgery, and she said, "You know, if my faith can't sustain me now, then my faith isn't any good." Then she referred to Psalm 139, her favorite chapter in the Bible. Of course, I knew what she was thinking. Verse 16 says, "You saw me before I was born. Every day of my life was recorded in your book. Every moment was laid out before a single day had passed." Without saying it, we knew this might be Barb's final day. Then David continued: "How precious are your thoughts about me, O God. They cannot be numbered! I can't even count them; they outnumber the grains of sand! And when I wake up, you are still with me!" And when her spirit was released from a surgery her body did not survive, she found God was still with her.

I had about four hours to be alone with God in that Toyota Rav 4 after our last conversation—four hours to talk, pray, cry, and think about His love. As I did, my mind wandered over to Habakkuk 3:17-19. Habakkuk had just learned from God that the Babylonians would one day invade Israel and take her people captive. After processing the worst news ever, Habakkuk wrote, "I trembled inside when I heard this; my lips quivered with fear. My legs gave way beneath me, and I shook in terror. I will wait quietly for the coming day when disaster will strike the people who invade us."

I understood his response. I was facing the worst news ever in a parking garage in Tulsa. However, that was not the part of Habakkuk's words that gave me strength. It was his next words that determined the direction which, in that moment, I chose to take in my relationship with God.

Habakkuk wrote, "Even though the fig trees have no blossoms, and there are no grapes on the vines; even though the olive crop fails, and the fields lie empty and barren; even though the flocks die in the fields, and the cattle barns are empty, yet I will rejoice in the Lord! I will be joyful in the God of my salvation! The Sovereign Lord is my strength! He makes me as surefooted as a deer, able to tread upon the heights." In other words, faith ensures that we will not lose our footing even when disaster strikes.

****

Around 1980, my friend Janet lost her sister to cancer. She was incredibly mad at God for allowing her sister to die, and she told Him so. She went boldly (this word in Hebrews 4:16 means "freedom of speech") before His throne of grace and loudly proclaimed her anger at

His injustice. After venting her displeasure with God, Janet sensed the Lord speak to her heart. He said, "You are angry at Me for taking her away, but not once have you thanked Me for the time you had with her."

Janet repented of her attitude, and she felt God's love and peace. By God's loving mercy, that conversation stayed with me for forty years, and little did I know I'd need it on a lonely Saturday evening in a parking garage in Tulsa, Oklahoma.

As I sat in the car thinking of Barbara, Habakkuk, and Jesus in Gethsemane, I said to God, "I pray for my wife's healing, Lord. But not my will, but yours be done."

And the tears began to flow. I took a big breath and continued, saying, "Lord, I'm making you a promise. If you take Barbara home, like Habakkuk I will choose to rejoice. Like my friend Janet, I will choose to thank you for all the days we had and I will never complain about all the days we didn't have."

At some point in our Christian walk, we must decide if God is truly sovereign. If I ask, "Is God sovereign over principalities and the spiritual powers that be?" some would say, "Of course!" If I were to ask, "Is He sovereign over world affairs?" others might say, "After watching the news lately, I hope so." If I ask, "Is He sovereign over our dreams and desires?" a few people might think I was getting a bit too personal. If I ask, "Is God sovereign over our pain and happiness?" then some might not like the direction this conversation is going. Now, the question of the moment is this: is God sovereign over life and death?

As I sat in that parking garage, I decided that if God is not 100% sovereign in my life, He is not my Sovereign Lord at all. Psalm 139:5-6 says, "You go before me and follow me. You place your hand of blessing on my head. Such knowledge is too wonderful for me, too great for me to understand!" I knew I could not tell God I was thankful for all the time I had with Barbara and then tell Him I was upset at the time we didn't have. I understood if that were my attitude, God would no longer be sovereign over my past and my future.

Therefore, on Saturday, September 12, 2020, I made a decision to rejoice in God, come what may, and what did come altered my world.

Author Dallas Willard says that any thought about God that is not good and magnificent is heretical. Because of my faith and daily trust in God, I choose to remember His magnificence. Is it easy? No. Does it feel like a piece of my soul has been ripped out? Yes, because it has.

Genesis 2:18 says God knew it was not good for Adam to be alone. "I will make a helper who is just right for him," God says. In His creation of Eve, Genesis 2:21-22 says God "took out one of Adam's ribs." Most contemporary scholars agree a better translation might be, "and God took a part of the man's side." Therefore, since Barbara's death it feels like half of me is gone. The beautiful lady who was "just right" for me is no longer by my side. The pain is deep because the love is deep.

I've discovered that my life in the last forty days has taken a simple course: one breath forward and two tears back, and I find I'm still gaining. God doesn't count progress like we do. It's called grace, and it's a lesson that can only be learned in a difficult season.

So, here is my prayer for all of us who have experienced unimaginable pain through a loss. It is a prayer to have and to hold onto, from this day forward, for better and for worse, for richer and for poorer, in sickness and in health, till death do us part. And I hope it will be your prayer, too.

"Yet I will rejoice in the Lord! I will be joyful in the God of my salvation! The Sovereign Lord is my strength!"

"No one is to pursue what he judges better for himself, but instead, what he judges better for someone else."

<small>BENEDICT OF NURSIA</small>

My Pain Is Not
Your Problem

AS I HEADED out of Independence for Tulsa, I left a voice message with my bishop, Randell Drake, telling him I was on my way to St. John's where Barbara was scheduled for surgery. I told him to pray and, since he lived in the area, hinted I might need a place to spend the night. He never responded, which surprised me. However, I knew the bishop could be a very busy man. This silence from Bishop Drake turned out to be the hand of God.

Before the doctors finished working on Barbara, I received a call from one of the surgeons, who told me they were having difficulty removing the clots from her leg. He also told me her heart had stopped beating during surgery, and they spent thirty minutes massaging it before it started beating again. I asked him if there would be any damage to her brain, but he said there were too many drugs in her system to know. He would call me in about fifteen minutes as they were now finishing the surgery.

Fifteen minutes slowly passed. An hour later, a nurse called and asked me to come to a room on the third floor. She told me to check in with security and someone would escort me upstairs. As I sat there in the conference room, I instinctively knew what had happened and, when the doctors came in, the look on their faces confirmed it. They told me about something called "COVID lung," which had produced clots in Barbara's heart and leg. The doctors said the surgery had involved going in through her femoral artery to remove the clots from her leg and foot, but her heart simply couldn't endure the trauma, and Barbara had passed away on the table.

After the doctors left, two nurses in their twenties came into the room to sit with me. They needed to know what funeral home I wanted to use, my address, and a few other issues I don't remember. As they gently asked me these questions, I did my best to answer calmly through the tears quickly welling up in my eyes. Eventually, I asked them if they had been in surgery with Barbara; they had. It gave me comfort to sit with two gentle women who were the last to see Barbara alive.

"Thank you for all you did for my wife," I said. "You would have really liked her." One of the nurses left to process my information, leaving the other with me. Smiling, she asked, "May I pray with you?"

"Oh yes, please!" I said. "I am a pastor in Independence, so I know what that means. But before you do, may I ask you a question? This may sound strange or inappropriate, so you can say no."

I paused because I didn't know how to express what I wanted. I fumbled around for a moment, tried to focus on the floor, cried some more and then finally looked this sweet nurse in the eyes and said, "Can I get a hug?"

She smiled and said, "Of course," so we stood up and hugged. It was then, feeling the gentle contact of another person for the first time in twelve hours, that I heaved and sobbed and cried out loud on her shoulder. It was a release I so desperately needed but had to hold back until all the questions were asked and answered.

Now I didn't need to hold back. I don't remember ever crying and sobbing that hard in my life.

Finally, a nurse brought me a bag containing the few items Barb had brought with her to the hospital: the clothes she had on (which still smelled like her), her phone (which we had our last conversation on), a headband (which she was fond of), her glasses (which I watched her put on every morning), and her wedding ring (which I put on her finger). A nurse walked me to the elevators and through the closed waiting room. I felt dazed as I exited through the glass doors leading to the parking garage and started up the ramp to the car. I was supposed to leave with my wife, but all I had in my hand was a plastic bag with the possessions she no longer needed.

Dr. Alix Oreck, the advising physician while Barbara was in the emergency room, is also a friend of mine, and it was she who had directed us to St. John's in Tulsa. She also kept in contact with me throughout the day. During one conversation, she asked me if I was returning to Independence, and I said yes, because my pillow was only an hour-and-a-half away. I had figured that once I knew Barbara was okay, I could simply drive home. Besides, the next day was Sunday, and I'm the pastor. However, I'm also cheap and didn't want to waste money on a hotel room! Ten minutes later, Alix sent me a text with a confirmation number for a hotel she had booked for me just a few miles away (my doctor was smarter than I was and knew what I needed when I didn't). Alone with Barbara's bag, I drove toward the hotel.

Trying to see the road through the tears, I called Bishop Drake again. This time he answered and was completely shocked to hear Barbara passed away. He never received the voicemail I had left on his phone that morning. The last he had heard, Barbara and I were both fine and looking forward to celebrating our eleventh anniversary as pastors of Journey Church on Sunday. He offered to be with me on my first Sunday without Barbara. I thought that would be a great idea.

Arriving at the hotel, I retrieved my overnight bag and—dazed—slowly walked in. I showed the girl at the desk my confirmation number on my phone, and she turned to look it up on the computer. Then she looked at me and said, "I don't find that number."

"Well," I said, "a friend made the reservation. Perhaps it is under my name: Thornber." She turned and tried again, but still found no confirmation number.

Flustered but in cheerful spirits, she asked her manager for help. The manager came over, gave her some instructions and, of course, found the reservation. The girl looked up at me, smiled, and said, "I'm sorry. This is my first day."

I suppose I would have been within my emotional rights to lash out at this first-day-on-the-job clerk and hiss, "Don't you know my wife just died? Can't you see I'm exhausted and an emotional wreck? Don't you know what I've been through? Get your act together! Learn your job or find another place to work!"

> While in the midst of our most devastating pain, we can still exhibit the kindness and compassion of Christ.

Given the circumstances, I'm sure most people would have understood my reaction and given me the leeway to be rude.

But, from somewhere in the depths of my weariness, I, too, managed a smile. "That's okay," I said. "Everyone has a first day on the job."

As soon as I said that, I sensed God speak these

words into my heart: "Very good, son. Your pain is not her problem."

I wish I knew how I managed that response. I think Barb would've been proud.

Choosing not to respond with sometimes-justifiable anger is a decision. So is choosing joy. While in the midst of our most devastating pain, we can still exhibit the kindness and compassion of Christ, because He set the example for us from the Cross. He not only forgave His executioners, but He also brought one more sinner into the Kingdom and took care of the needs of His mother. His pain did not give Him permission to be unkind. Neither did mine.

As I tried to fall asleep that first night, alone with my thoughts about my Barbara who was no longer by my side, I closed my eyes and said, "I'm ready, Lord. It's okay if you take me home tonight, too. I'm done." When I woke up in the morning (disappointed, I'll confess), I thought, "I'm still breathing, so God isn't finished with me yet." At that moment, I made a decision to live.

When asked how I manage to stay positive with God, even when He allowed Barbara to die, I can only say, "I have chosen joy in a time of sorrow." I maintain my faith in the magnificent goodness of our Sovereign

God because of a decision I made alone in a parking garage, waiting for news about my wife.

Around 4:30 a.m. I got back in the car and drove home. After I parked the car, I sat a while longer, not wanting to walk into a house in which everything would remind me of Barbara. I just stared at the sidewalk that led to a house that was no longer our home. Reluctantly, I went in and, after wandering around for a while, started to get dressed for church. While I was putting on my shoes, Bishop Drake called me. "Jim, you'll never guess what happened. I did get your voicemail…at six-thirty this morning!"

I'm convinced God delayed that voicemail to Bishop Drake so I could spend time alone with Him in my car. God gave me time to contemplate my life with or without Barbara, how I was going to respond to God, how I was going to live after her death. If Bishop Drake had been sitting with me in that Toyota Rav 4, I would never have talked to God the way I did, and I may have not promised to rejoice in His sovereign goodness.

I thank God my bishop didn't pick up the phone.

I thank God He has never left me alone.

"When we are stunned to the place beyond words, when an aspect of life takes us away from being able to chip away at something until it's down to a manageable size and then to file it nicely away, when all we can say in response is 'Wow,' that's a prayer."

ANNE LAMOTT

(Anne Lamotte, *Help, Thanks, Wow: The Three Essential Prayers,* Riverhead Books, 2012, pg. 73.)

The "WOW" Factor

FIVE DAYS AFTER Barbara died, I was driving home from Arkansas after spending time with the kids and grandkids. As I neared Cassville, Missouri, I thought of Barbara and my eyes were wet. I don't recommend driving through the Ozark Mountains when you're having trouble seeing the road, but there I was, remembering our adventures as a couple—the places we traveled to, the lives we touched, the way our family has grown—and out of my mouth came, "Wow, God! What a great life we had!" Immediately my spirit felt as if someone had reached in and lifted off a weight, like the ones on a barbell at a gym. So, I tried it again.

"Wow, God, we had such a wonderful relationship!" Again, lightness.

"Wow, God, thank you for trusting me with Your daughter for over twenty-six years, especially at the last when she needed me the most!" Tears. Joy.

Then I started to have fun with the word, "Wow." That could stand for "Wonderfully Outrageous Woman," and that made me smile, so I tried it again. "Wildly Obedient Wife!" And that made me laugh out loud. Wild? She had her moments. Obedient wife? Sure, mostly. And the lightness continued as I drove north out of Cassville.

> Joy is not opposed to mourning.

Maybe it seems strange that I made W.O.W. an acronym for something, but I needed to laugh. More importantly, in those moments I discovered that joy is not opposed to mourning. I can still find humor and joy in life even when my heart is heavy, and I can still be happy and cheer for others when I don't feel cheerful myself.

A few days before I started writing this book, I stood at the paint counter where I work my second job and an elderly couple, perhaps in their late eighties, walked by me holding hands. I'll confess that my first thought was about myself, how I will never have a relationship that will last that long. I won't have Barbara's hand to hold when we are in our eighties. But that thought only lasted a moment because I found myself smiling at them, rejoicing that they still had one another.

The Apostle Paul writes, "Rejoice with those who rejoice; mourn with those who mourn" (Rom. 12:15). My current state of mourning is not opposed to rejoicing when I see goodness and joy in others. I can still say "Wow" when I'll never experience that joy myself. However, sometimes I need reminders to be grateful.

I attended a pastors' retreat in Rome, Georgia, last year, where author and fellow minister Gary Moon spoke. The theme of this retreat was Relationship Building and Spiritual Formation, and Gary taught us how to be more aware of the presence of God. One practice Gary observed was to set his phone to ping every three hours during the day as a reminder to center his thoughts on God. I thought that was a great idea, and now my phone vibrates and sounds a small alarm five times a day at 8, 10, 12, 2, and 4 o'clock.

Many times, of course, when that alarm pings, I find my mind has wandered into places that do not bring glory to God, so I retreat and thank God for His love and forgiveness. Other times, the alarm catches me in a conversation with someone, so I say a silent prayer for them without their knowledge. Sometimes, I dedicate these five prayer times to one individual, anticipating the alarm and asking God how I should pray for them at this hour. At the end of the day, I tell them how I prayed for them, and it becomes a way for me to build our relationship.

My phone still gives me those reminders, but now I dedicate those times to saying "Wow" and expressing my gratitude to God—gratitude not just for what I had with Barbara, but for what I have today. Fortunately, this choice to express gratitude is a habit Barbara and I formed years ago.

Just as Barbara was a morning person, so am I. Because I am a bi-vocational pastor who also writes out his sermons, my sermon preparation starts on Monday morning. The alarm goes off at 4 a.m., and by 4:30 a.m. I'm in my study, hitting on all eight cylinders, digging into the Word and creating my next sermon. Before Barbara's death, I would leave my study at 5:45 a.m. and meet her in the living room, where we would talk about what we were studying, discuss our day, and pray together.

One morning, I shared with her a question I read during my study time: "What if you woke up today with only the things you thanked God for yesterday?" That quote in various configurations has been all over the Internet, so I have no idea where it originated, but I do know it struck a chord with us. From that day forward, gratitude became central to our morning times together. It's also what makes it so easy for me to say "Wow" when my phone alarm goes off, for gratitude became a habit long before I ever imagined how much I'd need it.

> Gratitude became a habit long before I ever imagined how much I'd need it.

In her 1969 book *On Death and Dying*, Elisabeth Kübler-Ross says those experiencing grief experience five stages of emotions: denial, anger, bargaining, depression, and acceptance. Because her death happened so fast, I didn't have time to experience and work through those five valid stages of grief. Perhaps what Kübler-Ross failed to encounter in her studies were people whose faith in a magnificent God was central to their lives. It is this faith that allowed me to jump over her five emotional stages while I sat alone in a parking garage in Tulsa and land squarely on what I call the sixth stage: Gratitude. Now, with each ping of my phone, the "Wow Factor" continues.

Another "Wow" moment came six days after Barbara passed. For about ten years, I've been having coffee on Friday mornings with a group of pastors from different denominations in Independence. Because we've become friends on a social basis, we see ourselves as companions, not competitors, in our Kingdom work. I knew I would need their friendship, compassion, and wisdom, so I sent a text to the group telling them I would be there Friday and could use their presence. Pastors from the Assemblies of God, Nazarene, Baptist, Lutheran, and Friends Church were among those who showed up. It was wonderful.

I told them about my time in the parking garage where I decided to worship God who is sovereign over my past and my future. I said, "I cannot thank Him for what I had and at the same time be angry that I didn't have more time with Barbara, for then He stops being sovereign."

John Penrose, from the Evangelical Friends Church, said, "That's right. Besides, how much more time would have been enough?"

"Wow. You're right," I said. "Would three more years have been enough? Would fifteen more years have been enough?"

"That's why we look forward to eternity," John said. "Only eternity with our loved ones is enough."

Because Barbara and I had already formed a habit of expressing our gratitude for God's magnificence, that trait sustained me when she died. I did not have to desperately manufacture it. When I play boogie-woogie on the piano, my left hand moves from muscle memory gained through years of practice. I don't have to think about playing every note, for my fingers move naturally along the keyboard. In the same way, gratitude is at its best when we exercise it from spiritual memory—a natural response gained from years of practice.

Paul says, "Clothe yourself with the presence of the Lord Jesus Christ" (Rom. 13:14), and he writes to the Philippians, "You must have the same attitude that Christ Jesus had" (Phil. 2:5). Putting on the mind of Christ is a choice, like deciding which pair of socks to wear when I get dressed. When the channel of my mind begins to wander like a distant AM station, I adjust the dial of my thoughts until I'm tuned into the clarity of God's thoughts, and slowly but perceptively, the static of Jim's thoughts fades away. Choosing to think of the goodness of God always produces a "Wow" factor in my heart, and I smile once again.

"You will never forget the hurts, Gary, but you can draw strength from where you've been. With this strength you can comfort others. And as you comfort others, you will heal more."

—Dr. Jeremiah Donigian
to Medal of Honor recipient Gary Beikirch

(Marcus Brotherton, *Blaze of Light*, WaterBrook, 2020, p. 224.)

Bearing My Brother's Burden

SEVENTEEN DAYS AFTER Barbara passed away, I received a call from my friend, Mike. Due to the advanced stages of cancer, his wife, Michelle, was on hospice care. A little over three years earlier, I had the privilege of marrying Mike and Michelle at Journey Church. Since they had both been previously married, this was a sweet, simple, sacred, and beautiful ceremony of two people in their forties once again finding love and rejoicing in God's blessings.

Naturally, Mike first gave me his condolences about Barbara. He thanked me for our last conversation in the frozen foods section of Wal-Mart, where I offered the best comfort I could about Michelle—only one day before Barbara died.

Then Mike said, "I hate to bring it up at this time, but I was wondering if you could come out and visit with Michelle sometime soon. You know, whenever you get a chance."

"I'll see you tomorrow," I told him.

As we stood in Michelle's room, I told Mike that Journey Church was available to him and the family for any arrangements they wanted to make. Then we all prayed together and I drove back to work.

> Just because I'm in pain doesn't mean others are not.

When some of my friends learned that I took time off from work to visit Michelle, they looked at me in amazement and shook their heads. Some of them wondered how Mike could make such a request of me so soon after Barbara's death, while others asked me how I had the strength to visit Michelle for the same reason.

The only answer I can give to those questions is that I'm learning that pain does not discriminate. In other words, just because I'm in pain doesn't mean others are not. The world hasn't stopped spinning because I'm in mourning, and I am not unique. I'm not the first man on earth to lose his wife, and I have not earned special treatment because my heart is heavy. Of course, my friends and family treat me with the utmost care. However, this is their loving response to my pain and loss. It's not something I'm entitled to. Therefore, I'm grateful when love and compassion come my way.

About a week after I visited Mike and Michelle at their home, Michelle passed away. Mike called me while I was at work and asked me if I would officiate at her memorial, and of course, I said yes.

I took Mike's call while I was working in the back of Woods Lumber, surrounded by plastic totes full of the freight I was checking in. Slowly, I leaned forward and rested my arms on one of those totes. Mark Woods, the owner, happened to be in the back and caught the last part of the conversation. I told him I was going to do another memorial on Saturday for the wife of a friend. This would be my third memorial service in twenty-four days. He looked at me a bit shocked and said, "Do you need a hug or something?"

Truthfully, I didn't know how I was going to do another memorial so soon after losing Barb. As I gazed off into nothingness, I remembered that Galatians 6:2

says, "Bear one another's burdens, and so fulfill the law of Christ." Immediately, another thought occurred to me: "And there's no loophole in that verse." There's no asterisk after the name *"Christ"* that leads to a footnote which reads, "Unless, of course, you're hurting or it makes you uncomfortable or it's inconvenient or you've just lost your spouse." Being a disciple of Christ doesn't give us any wiggle room to set aside a passage of Scripture because it's hard.

Losing my best friend and soul mate is indescribably painful, but I'm not the only one who lost Barb. When I walked into church for worship practice the morning after Barbara died, the team was in tears. Deep, sobbing tears. They were trying to keep themselves busy by gathering the worship music and adjusting microphone stands, but they were a mess. We all were. I made it a point to go to each person and hug them as long as they wanted. And sometimes that hug lasted as long as I needed it. *Everyone* was crying, and I found myself a blubbering mess. But I also spoke encouragement to each team member. They all needed to know that I understood their pain, and I shared with them the different ways Barb was proud of them.

After church that day, I drove to Arkansas to be

with the kids and grandkids. Once again, I made it a point to hug everyone and try to bring them comfort, sharing with them Barb's unique love and appreciation for them. I'm sure it helped eventually, but at that moment we were all inconsolable. For the next hour, we sat on the porch, silent except for the muffled sobs, bearing together a burden beyond description. No one needs to hurt alone.

One of the ways I sense God's pleasure is by remembering I am not the only one in the room who is in pain. When I was writing Michelle's memorial, I sensed God speak to my heart. "Don't mention Barbara," He said. "This memorial isn't about you. It's about Michelle." Those words were a gentle reminder that when I offer to someone what small comfort I can, and take just a little bit of their burden into my own heart, I find myself a few steps further down the path of my own healing process.

"Whoever does not see God everywhere

does not see Him anywhere."

Kotzker Rebbe

Creating Worship

WHEN I WAS about seven, a traveling salesman talked my parents into leasing an accordion so little Jimmy could learn to play an instrument. My dad was a drummer in his youth, but he gave it up after my younger sister was born. Time and a lack of money in a growing household didn't allow him to keep playing. I have only one memory of him sitting at his drums, but he kept a couple sets of drumsticks and a practice pad in the house, which let him keep a beat to one of his favorite Chuck Berry or Fats Domino albums. He even taught me to play different beats on his practice pad, which is probably why he thought my learning an instrument was a good idea.

Unfortunately, the traveling salesman somehow

failed to point out that after a certain period of time, my parents would have to upgrade the accordion to a much more expensive instrument if I were to continue getting lessons from the accordion company. It was more money than my parents wanted to invest, and I'm sure no one in the family was very happy with the squeaky noise of my practicing. Thus ended little Jimmy's accordion career. My mom's Jewish grandparents, may their memory be a blessing, stepped in and offered to buy us a piano if I thought I'd like to learn to play. I said yes and have been playing ever since.

Today when people hear me play, they compliment me on my talent. That always embarrasses me because I know I'm not a natural musician. I play as well as I do not because of talent, but through a combination of drive, dedication, and decades of practice. In other words, I've simply become proficient.

Today, this hard-won, acquired skill allows me to sit at the piano, close my eyes, and improvise through different chords, timings, and keys. I've been improvising like this for years, and it is my favorite way to worship God. However, even though I play piano on the worship team, I don't find this to be a relaxing, worshipful experience. Because I need music and chords to play the songs, while everyone else in church is worshiping, lifting their hands and enjoying the presence of God, I'm concentrating on the chords and the signals from my worship leader, telling me where we're going next in the song.

Therefore, my most intimate time of worship is when I'm alone at the piano. This time is intentional and spontaneous, gentle and inventive, and it never sounds the same way twice. It is also an emotional experience for me as I sit and play for God—just the two of us with nobody else in the room.

Then I married Barbara.

About two years after we married, I found myself alone in the house one day and sat down to improvise my worship. A little while later Barbara came home, walked in the door, and I immediately stopped playing.

"Don't stop," she said. "That's beautiful."

"Thank you," I replied, "but it wasn't for you. It was for God."

Barbara understood. She said being in the room when I played that way would be like watching a couple having a physically intimate moment together. Spectators are not allowed.

Years later, however, Barbara confessed she cheated

on me. One day she came home from the store and heard me playing. Knowing I'd stop if she came in the house, she sat on the front porch and listened. It makes me smile thinking of her sitting on the concrete steps, surrounded by groceries, closing her eyes and listening to her husband create loving harmonies for his Lord. She told me later, "When I realized the ice cream was starting to melt, I knew I had to go in the house and I knew you'd stop playing, and you did."

> "We cannot attain the presence of God because we're already totally in the presence of God."
>
> RICHARD ROHR

For the first month after Barbara died, I avoided playing the piano in the house. I still played for the worship team, but as I said, that is not a worshipful time for me. Playing alone is, and I avoided it because I knew how emotionally charged it would be. In his book *What the Mystics Know*, Richard Rohr writes, "We cannot attain the presence of God because we're already totally in the presence of God. What's absent is awareness."[1]

---

[1] Richard Rohr, *Everything Belongs: The Gift of Contemplative Prayer*, Crossroad; Revised and updated edition (March 1, 2003), pg. 29.

I understood that God was with me. What I avoided, however, was a deeper awareness of His goodness and love because I knew it would wreck me. That's why, for a month after Barbara died, I walked around the piano but never sat down. I'd look at it, know I needed to play it, but also know what it would do to me—and move on.

Then one day, the time came. I looked at the picture of us on our wedding day that hangs on the wall above the piano. In it, my hand cradles her chin while we look lovingly into one another's eyes. With a sigh, I sat down and played. I didn't want to, but I needed to.

The tears flowed, my nose ran, and soon, horrible, guttural wailing sounds welled from my chest to my mouth. I hung my head and continued crying as I created music for my Lord. My heart broke again as I realized how, for the first time, I was also playing for Barbara.

After I finished playing and blew my nose through a box of Kleenex, I sent a text to my friend and fellow musician, Julia Valentine, who lost her husband three years earlier. "I finally improvised on the piano," I wrote. "Cried harder than I ever have. Barb's death is four weeks ago tomorrow. Playing felt good and horrible and unspeakable at the same time."

Julia wrote back, "So good to crawl into the Father's lap. I am happy for this step taken in His perfect timing, and I am praying for your journey. Lots of growth, lots of tears, and learning to accept feeling uncomfortable."

A few days later, I received a call from Dr. Lou Shirey, Director of Thriving in Ministry program for the International Pentecostal Holiness Church. I told him about finally worshiping at the piano and he said, "I'm so glad you shared this with me, Jim. It is not the first time I've heard that." Dr. Shirey went on to tell me he has heard from several people who experienced deep loss, and those areas that once brought much joy to them temporarily dried up. He related how two writers told him that the words for writing "went out of them." He knows of another pastor/musician who took some time before he could play the guitar again. One pastor related to him that his joy was preparing sermons. After the death of his wife, he took two years to return to the joy of sermon preparation. All that time he continued to preach (and did so effectively) but the preparation was a grind for him.

Pastor and author John W. Stevenson says we are "worshipers by design." I'm convinced that honoring God with our designed, creative side is a primary act of worship. Our God is a creative God, for the first book of the Bible opens with God's creative activities. Because God also made us in His image, He gives us a variety of creative gifts so we may honor Him, worship Him, and imitate His creativity. This creative worship can be anything, for Ecclesiastes says, "Whatever your hand finds to do, do it with all your might" (9:10). Painting a picture, writing a children's book, planting a garden, restoring a car, knitting a blanket, baking a cake, even playing the piano are all acts of worship when we do them with an awareness of God's presence.

One of God's most generous gifts to us is the desire to create something where there once was nothing, just like He did. And when we do this in our grief and sorrow, we will find it to be a most amazing time of worship and thanksgiving.

"When we are no longer able to change a situation...we are challenged to change ourselves."

VIKTOR FRANKL

(Victor Frankl, *Man's Search for Meaning*, 1959-2006, Beacon Press, p. 112.)

"How Are You?"

SHORTLY AFTER I finished writing a few chapters of this book, I emailed a friend in the publishing business and told him what I was doing. After some back and forth communication, he wrote, "In some part of the book be willing to share how it feels when others respond to you in certain ways. I think most of us are never really sure what to say or how to act around someone who has just faced a deep loss, disappointment, or setback. I think you could write about that and it would be helpful."

Because I've never been known for my extreme subtlety nor my bashfulness, I'm not sure I'm the right person to offer advice about this subject. Too often, especially in my younger days, I was more likely to let my tongue wag before my brain had a chance to engage. That can still happen! Fortunately, with much training—accompanied with "that look" I'd get from Barbara—I've learned a modicum of social grace, much to the blessed relief of my family and friends. And yes, I'm still learning.

Since Barbara died, I've found myself having to respond to people who don't really know how to respond to me, and I understand. I don't know of any college that offers a course called "How to Talk to Someone Who Loses a Spouse and Not Sound Stupid." And even if such a class existed, I know I would not have signed up. This means most of us find ourselves caught like a squirrel crossing the road when a car is coming. We know we should do something but we can't make up our minds, and sometimes we end up getting flattened by an issue bigger than ourselves.

If you've lost someone, or if you know someone who has suffered a loss, you've probably said or heard one of the following:

How are you?

I can't imagine.

I'm praying for you.

Let me know if there is anything I can do.

I don't know what to say.

I'm going to go through each of these, first giving you my "before my brain gets engaged" initial response, followed by how I've learned to reply that is more in tune with the spirit of Jesus than the pain of Jim. What has helped me learn to respond in a loving, kind way is to remember that the people who approach me are already uncomfortable, out of their element, and for the most part want to love me but don't know how. I choose to remember that my pain is not their problem, and kindness is a fruit of the Spirit.

> I choose to remember that my pain is not their problem, and kindness is a fruit of the Spirit.

How are you?

My initial response: "How do you think? I just lost my wife!"

That's about as subtle as the Normandy Invasion. And it is certainly not kind.

How I reply: "Better with every breath," or "There are sad days and there are better days."

Both responses communicate to them, and remind me, that I'm healing but not healed. I also remind myself if someone has taken the difficult initiative to walk across the room and speak to me, they do so because they care. My family and friends ask, "How are you?" from the depths of their heart, and I truly appreciate it. However, people I count as acquaintances but not friends have said, "Sorry to hear about your wife," or "You have my condolences." All I need to say to them is, "Thank you."

I can't imagine

My initial response: "You're right. Don't even try!"

This would be Jim's selfish way of telling people that if personal pain were an Olympic event, I'd win. That response would make it look like I had some superhero amount of anguish they'd never comprehend. I'm glad those words have never come out of my mouth, and I'm still embarrassed I have even thought them in the first place. However, I cannot control my feelings. I can only control my actions.

How I reply: "I hope you never have to."

I cannot express how strongly I believe that. I wouldn't wish this pain on my worst enemy. I wish no one would ever again experience this amount of anguish and loss, but that's not reality. Everyone dies, so losing a loved one is a common experience. I can only hope the couples I know who have the loving relationship Barbara and I shared are fortunate enough to die together in bed, holding one another close.

I'm praying for you

My initial response: "I have no idea how prayer is going to help."

How I reply: "Thank you."

I remember the specific time someone said "I'm praying for you" at church the day after Barbara died. After I said, "Thank you," I gazed off towards the back of the church and, fighting a headache from crying so much, foggy from an awful, fitful four hours of sleep, I simply could not comprehend how, at that moment when I was just struggling to exist, prayer was going to make a difference.

Rather cynical for a pastor, isn't it?

Still, because I believe in prayer, I know it has helped in ways I may never fully understand. Besides, perhaps prayer is the only gift someone has to offer me. A person on a fixed income can't afford to cook me a meal, much less take me out to dinner. My neighbor who doesn't have a car can't volunteer to shop for me, but she has offered me her prayers.

When I pause long enough to think about it, what could be better than someone having a talk with God about me, asking Him to comfort me in my time of sorrow? That is such a gift of love and compassion. Someone is presenting my needs before the Throne of God. Isn't that magnificent?

Let me know if there's anything you need

My initial response: "I don't know what I need. Oh, yes I do. I NEED BARBARA BACK!"

How I reply: "I will. Thank you."

Thinking straight and knowing what I needed took time. When Bishop Drake offered to be with me at church the day after Barbara's death, I paused before I said yes. I was trying to decide if I needed his presence. I had just spent hours alone with God, and I thought I would be okay without my bishop with me. Then I heard Barb's often-repeated advice: "Let people help you." Slowly, I'm learning what I need. Even when I don't know I need something, like an invitation to dinner or a friend offering to accompany me to the funeral home to pick up Barbara's ashes, I say, "Thank you for your offer. Yes, I'd like that." So far, that "Yes" has worked out well every time.

Now that I'm not as raw and emotional as I was in the first week, when someone says, "Let me know if there's anything you need," I say, "I need someone to help me pay off my mortgage." That initially catches them off guard, then they smile, and we end up laughing together. Sometimes laughter is the medicine I need the most, but I'm still open to help regarding the mortgage.

I don't know what to say

Surprisingly, I've never imagined a negative response to this statement. The first time someone said this to me I replied, "You don't have to say anything. I appreciate your love and concern." Other times, in order to relieve the obvious tension, I'll continue by saying, "Barb was a great wife and we had a great life." I know that won't work for every loss we face, but it's my way of showing appreciation to those who simply want to comfort me and don't know how.

Gam Zu l'tovah

"This too is for the good."

<small>JEWISH PROVERB</small>

Goodness and Tears

BARBARA AND I were fond of going to the Farmer's Market in Independence. She even set up a table a few times and sold some of her garden plates and the creations she made with shells we picked up when we visited her mom in Newport Beach, California. Even if we didn't need anything, we liked to go to the market and wander around.

One Thursday evening at the Farmer's Market we saw a table where a family was selling coffee they roasted at their home. We struck up a delightful conversation, learned their names—Erika and Jason—talked about the different types of coffee we liked, and bought a pound of whole bean coffee to grind as our weekend treat. This coffee is so good it turned me away from the international brand I'd been grinding for over thirty years. On our next visit to their stall at the Farmer's Market, we proudly told Erika and Jason we had switched to their coffee.

About two weeks after Barbara died, I visited Erika's stall to pick up another pound of coffee. She told me how shocked she was upon hearing of Barbara's death and that she'd been following me on Facebook. It was a gentle, compassionate conversation. So far, so good.

> It was just a bag of coffee! But it was so much more.

I thanked her for her kind words and reached into my pocket for my wallet to pay for the coffee. Erika said, "No. When I read about Barbara, I knew I wanted to do something for you, so this coffee is a gift."

That's when the tears started to flow and I lost it. That simple act of kindness set me off, and I was quite surprised. It was just a bag of coffee! But it was so much more. I looked at Erika, speechless, and leaned forward to give her a hug. As other customers gathered around, I managed to say, "I'm sorry. I need to go. Thank you!" Erika smiled and I walked a not very straight line back to the car.

Talk show host and author Dennis Prager once said on his radio program, "When I was younger, evil made me cry. Now that I am older, evil makes me angry and goodness makes me cry." I didn't completely understand that statement until I had an encounter with a beautiful soul and received the free gift of a pound of coffee.

Another frequent source of my tears is my church. They have rallied around me in so many wonderful ways I cannot begin to count them all. Their gentleness, sincere interest in my well-being, prayers and kindness have been a healing medicine to my broken heart.

Across our nation, October is Pastor Appreciation Month, and my church made sure they appreciated me. Every Sunday in October they presented me with a little gift. I always find this month to be somewhat embarrassing, but I know they needed to say "thank you" to me, just as I needed to say "thank you" to them.

One Sunday after receiving one of their gifts, I realized they were not just thanking me, they were thanking Barbara, also. For some reason I decided I would try to tell them how much their love meant, how much Barbara would appreciate them, how much we all missed her. I got about four words into my impromptu speech and choked up, once again finding myself speechless.

The congregation smiled at me and waited while I cried, walked in a circle, took a sip of water, looked helplessly back at them, and waited for the tears to stop. I was so glad when Meagan, our worship leader, walked to the front of the church and gave me a big hug saying, "I couldn't stand it anymore and had to hug you."

Such goodness. Such tears.

****

It's November 7, and I just finished cleaning out Barbara's pride-and-joy flower garden in the backyard. I've been avoiding this task, as every part of the garden speaks of her love and generosity. The only flowers she liked to grow were flowers she could cut, arrange, and give away, with zinnias and gladioluses being her favorites. She would often make flower arrangements for the communion table at church, and after the service, she would take those arrangements to someone who was sick or simply needed to know we were thinking about them. We spent many hours together in that flower garden, weeding, planting, talking, and watching the butterflies move from flower to flower. It was our place of peace.

After I bagged up all the dead stalks, I started to walk back towards the house. As I looked at the now-barren ground, I saw I had missed two new zinnias, about three inches high, poking through the ground. They even had the formation of little flower buds. In November! I was so excited about these little flower warriors soldiering on in spite of the coming winter, my first inclination was to take out my phone and send a picture to Barbara. Once again, the tears welled up in my eyes as I remembered there was no place for me to send it.

I've found I can rejoice in the beautiful life I had with Barbara and be grateful for the gifts of coffee and prayers, hugs and family, memories and friends. But I cannot choose when I cry.

However, next spring when the zinnias and gladioluses once again poke through the dirt after a long, hard winter, I'll think of Barbara and be glad that life continues.

Acknowledgments

THIS BOOK CAME about because two friends told me I had to write about the way I've handled my grief since Barbara passed away. The first is my friend Cece Helmers, whom I met when I was seventeen when she took over the youth group at the Foursquare Church our family attended in Thousand Oaks, California. When she first suggested I write this book, I told her I thought it was too soon and I didn't think I could do it. The second friend is Taylor Drake, who *insisted* I write another book. His enthusiasm, along with Cece's encouragement, helped me do what I didn't think was possible.

Because I didn't think this book was worth reading, I sent a rough draft of the only two chapters I'd written to my high school friend and fellow author Donna Jones. Her response was, "Holy cow!!!! This is WONDERFUL! You need to write this." Thank you, Donna, for cheering me onward.

I also want to thank Dr. Lou Shirey, Bishop Randell Drake, Taylor Drake, and Mike Masters for reading the manuscript and giving me wonderful advice. They helped me correct some grammar and offer insights about conversations I didn't remember clearly. Their leadership and friendship remains a steady foundation in my healing process.

I could not have completed this project without the continual love and support of our family after losing their daughter, mom, grandmother, sister, aunt, great-aunt, and sister-in-law. Barbara was our inspiration, cheerleader, friend, and champion—all the traits that live on because she taught us by example what it means to be a family. Thank you to the Shelleys, Browns, Blanchards, and Zells.

Thank you David Welday and the staff at HigherLife Publishing and Marketing. Their creativity and consistent push to finish in a timely matter brought this book into existence. It was a pleasure to work with you again.

I cannot say enough about the amazing editing of

the inimitable Debbie Pope. Her expert understanding of English, her copious notes written in red throughout the chapters, and her consistent comments ("Oxford comma." "You lost me here, Jim." "You changed tenses." "Subject/verbs must agree." "Conditional tense: if… were…not, if…was…" "Great phrasing!") had me feeling as if I failed my native language! However, it also helped this book to be better than I could ever write on my own. Thank you, Debbie.

Finally, a huge debt of thanks goes out to the friends I've known for years, friends I've recently met, and friends I hope to meet in person. There are too many to mention here, but if we've talked about Barb, grief, or the magnificent love and goodness of God; if you've sat with me, prayed, hugged, or wordlessly cried with me in any way since Barb's passing, you are a significant contributor to this book in ways you will never know.

About the Author

J IM THORNBER is the pastor of Journey Church in Independence, Kansas. In 1984, he graduated from Bethany Bible College in Scotts Valley, California, with a Bachelor of Science degree in Ministry. In 2007, he obtained a Master of Ministry degree in Leadership from the Graduate School at Southwestern Christian University in Bethany, Oklahoma. Jim's previous book, *Taking Off My Comfortable Clothes*, tells his story of joining a monastic community in Eureka Springs, Arkansas, where for four years he was a monk with The Brothers and Sisters of Charity at The Little Portion Hermitage, while still maintaining his ministerial credentials with the Assemblies of God.

IF YOU HAVE BEEN BLESSED BY THIS BOOK, WILL YOU HELP ME SPREAD THE WORD?

There are several ways you can help me get the word out about the message of this book…

- Post a 5-Star review on Amazon.
- Write about the book on your Facebook, Twitter, Instagram, LinkedIn – any social media you regularly use!
- If you blog, consider referencing the book, or publishing an excerpt from the book with a link back to my website. You have my permission to do this as long as you provide proper credit and backlinks.
- Recommend the book to friends – word-of-mouth is still the most effective form of advertising.
- Purchase additional copies to give away as gifts.

The best way to connect with me is at
jimthornber.com.

ENJOY ANOTHER TITLE BY JAMES THORNBER

Taking Off My Comfortable Clothes

Removing Religion to Find Relationship

A life of faith isn't lived in a neat, clean, stain-free environment; it's lived outside the familiar, in the center of the adventurous, untamed call of God on our lives. This intimate, soul-searching account describes Jim Thornber's remarkable journey to a living, loving God. It started with a search for something spiritually higher yet soulishly comfortable; something that would make him feel relevant and reasonable, giving him a purpose for living and a sense of calling. His search finally led him to remove the comfortable, religious misconceptions of who he thought he was (and who he thought God wanted him to be) and put on the clothes of Christ to find true relationship.

You can order these books from Amazon, Barnes & Noble, or wherever you purchase your favorite books.